Popular Concert Favorites

for
Bb Instruments

Clarinet	Trumpet	Tenor Sax
3242	3831	4212

Printed in Canada

COMPACT DISC PAGE AND BAND INFORMATION

Music Minus One

Popular Concert Favorites
Clarinet Trumpet Tenor Sax

MMO CD 3242
MMO CD 3831
MMO CD 4212

Sarabande

J. S. Bach (1685-1750)

Träumerei

Robert Schumann (1810-1856)

Tournament of Temperaments
1. The Melancholic

Ditters von Dittersdorf (1739-1799)

2. The Humble

MMO CD 3242
MMO CD 3831
MMO CD 4212

3. The Gentle

Solemn March

Felix Mendelssohn (1809-1847)

Moment musical

Franz Schubert (1797-1828)

Toreador Song

Georges Bizet (1838-1875)

Allegro molto moderato

MMO CD 3242
MMO CD 3831
MMO CD 4212

To a Wild Rose

Edward MacDowell (1860-1908)

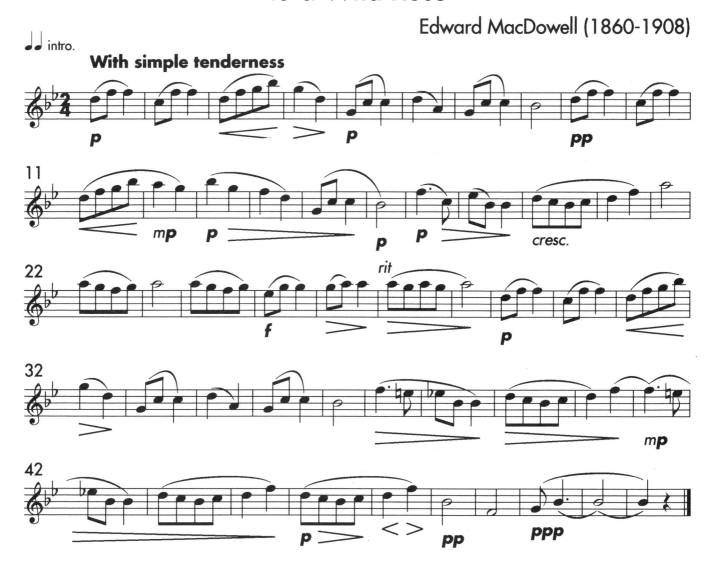

Prelude

Fryderyk Chopin (1810-1849)

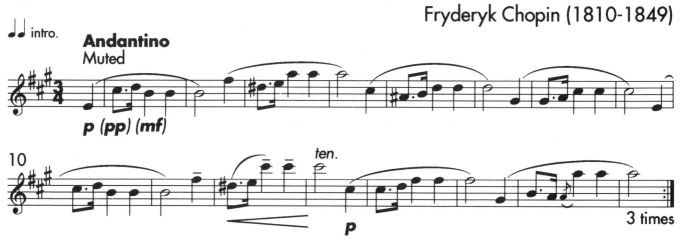

3 times

Triumphal March (from *Aida*)

Giuseppe Verdi (1813-1901)

MMO CD 3242
MMO CD 3831
MMO CD 4212

14

Popular Concert Favorites

for Bb Instruments

Clarinet	Trumpet	Tenor Sax
3242	3831	4212

 MUSIC MINUS ONE 50 Executive Boulevard • Elmsford New York 10523-1325